MAKE ME A COCKTAIL

AT CHRISTMAS

AUTHOR
NICK WILKINS

EDITOR
ASTRID BOWSER

PUBLISHED 2020
EDITION 2

INTRODUCTION

Cocktails are more than just a drink, they are delicious works of art crafted from a creative outlet to be savoured in the moment. We firmly believe that cocktails make great moments; a moment of creativity, a moment to share with others, a moment to give, a moment to relax, a moment to indulge and a moment to feel festive at Christmas.

Once you start making cocktails, the limits of your creativity are only governed by three things; your preferred tastes, your imagination and what ingredients you have in your cupboard and fridge! We hope that Make Me A Cocktail At Christmas gives you inspiration and confidence at home year after year to celebrate with your favourite tipples.

Christmas is our most favourite time of the year here at Make Me A Cocktail. We can justify making a decadent and creamy Brandy Alexander, indulge in a champagne based cocktail like the Limoncello Sparkle, get cosy in our pyjamas with a Hot Peppermint Patty or party with pals and a Christmas Punch. We have chosen an inspiring selection of cocktails to make for yourself and loved ones this Christmas, from famous cocktails to aperitifs with obligatory festive flavours to social media worthy winter works of art. How awesome is it that you can now make these delicious concoctions at home?!

We want to thank our friends and family for being the guinea pigs of both our cocktail making and book publication evolution, without whom we would not be able to improve on and be as proud of this, our third book, for you all to enjoy at Christmas!

Happy Holidays and happy cocktail making!

Nick and Astrid
Make Me A Cocktail

Makemeacocktail.com is the world's biggest and best cocktail resource! Over the years, the Make Me A Cocktail community has created and shared over 3,500 inspiring, classic and occasionally daring cocktail concoctions for fellow enthusiasts to recreate simply at home, for entertaining guests at parties or making memorable, unique events.

CONTENTS

2

GUIDE TO COCKTAIL CREATIVITY

Cocktails made by mixologists are works of art. Their flair, confidence, seamless choreography, finishing touches and presentation makes it feel impossible to recreate and look almost too good to drink. Almost...

The thing is, like painting a picture, anyone can have a go, it just takes a little practice and creativity to discover your own unique style! Throw the right proportions of the ingredients into a cocktail shaker with ice, shake a little then strain. You'll produce delicious cocktails time and time again. Garnish with an orange slice or a grating of nutmeg this Christmas and your friends will think you're the next Tom Cruise from that wonderful 80's film Cocktail. Run a lemon wedge round the rim of a glass and dip in green and red sugar crystals, sprinkle some cinnamon and you're the next world class bartender.

However, all drinks do need some basics to get you going. To get you started on your own creative journey at home, we list some basic equipment you'll need, plus some simple terminology and techniques to blaze your own path to cocktail stardom. Cocktails are to be enjoyed, so have fun and play with the flavours you've got to hand. You never know, you may create a new classic for the world to enjoy!

HOW TO USE THIS BOOK

We've broken down each recipe to be easy to follow and helpful in allowing you to create the perfectly balanced cocktail.

For each cocktail we've included the glass type we recommend, a small bit of background, the ingredients and method and also a 'difficulty rating' from 1 to 3. This rating is meant as a guide to the complexity of the creation, the time it takes to make or how much a small alteration in the recipe could affect the final outcome.

Where appropriate we've also included garnishes in the method. As with all cocktails, use your imagination and think what garnishes could work with a suitable cocktail. If you don't have a certain recommended garnish available, don't let that stop you from trying something similar, or something else that could compliment the flavour profile.

Where necessary we've also included little arrows to denote which picture relates to which cocktail.

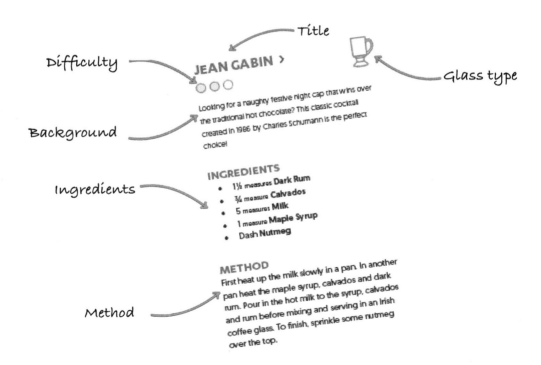

4

KEY INGREDIENTS

Just starting out on your cocktail journey, or want to know if you're missing out on a frequent ingredient that will open up a whole new world of flavour excitement? We're here to help.

There are some core ingredients most bars, household to professional, should include and we've listed these below. We recommend building up your collection with these key ingredients as a base to help you create a broad range of cocktails from the start!

SPIRITS

Start your collection off with these core bottles and you'll be creating wonderful cocktails in no time:

Vodka	Gin
White Rum	Tequila
Cointreau	Peach Schnapps
Amaretto	Champagne
Dark Rum	Whisky

MIXERS AND YOUR HOME CABINET

And just make sure you're stocked up with the following core home essentials:

Lemon Juice	Lime Juice
Orange Juice	Grenadine
Pineapple Juice	Sugar Syrup
Cranberry Juice	Lemonade
Angostura Bitter	Eggs

EQUIPMENT

COCKTAIL SHAKER

You can't get far with most cocktails without the staple of any personal home bar - the cocktail shaker. Add some ice to the ingredients within, shake for 10-15 seconds and strain into the required glass. Simple.

STRAINER

Right after the cocktail shaker comes the strainer. Some shakers have a basic strainer built in, but to catch all those ice lumps or fruit pieces you don't want in your finished product, a simple strainer suffices.

JIGGER

To get the right balance of flavors you need the right proportions of the ingredients, and most of the time that'll be in the form of measuring the liquid in a jigger. Most jiggers have a single and double measure top and bottom.

A GOOD GLASS

A good glass of the right size and shape for the recipe is the ideal finishing touch before enjoying a freshly prepared cocktail in the best way possible! The nicer looking the glass, the more photograph-worthy the finish!

TECHNIQUES

SHAKING

"Just make sure the top stays on" as my old bartending mentor used to say. I pass that knowledge onto you now. However with that pearl of wisdom, you'll want to break up the ice into smaller particles, chilling the contents and combining the flavors. Shaking for around 10-15 seconds is usually sufficient, you'll feel the outside of the shaker become cold and frosted.

STIRRING

I'm not sure we need to give you an introduction to what this means, but if you want to get all cocktail geeky, then stirring allows you to chill drinks, or combine flavors, without bubbling up or bruising the ingredients and doesn't dilute the drink from the ice as much as shaking does. It also allows you to mix fizzy elements such as champagne or soda. For a thorough stir, twizzle away for 10-15 seconds.

MUDDLING

Muddling - such a great descriptive word, literally muddling or mashing the flavors together. If you don't have one you don't need a muddler, the end of a small rolling pin will do the job just fine, but a muddler helps really release those flavors we want to taste in a cocktail. Simply grind and twist whatever you're muddling a few times to get the juices and oils released from the ingredients.

INGREDIENT SWITCHES

Although nothing beats following a recipe to the letter and make a cocktail exactly as the recipe creator intended, you should not deprive yourself of your creativity and making a great cocktail if you have a suitable alternative ingredient!

Think about the flavours in the recipe you want to try. Why not try an alternative spirit or liqueur with a similar flavor, for example Triple Sec instead of Cointreau? Prosecco instead of Champagne? Go wild and try vodka instead of gin – it'll be a riff on the cocktail but maybe you'll discover that new classic!

Also, why not try non-alcoholic versions? There are some incredible alternatives to having alcohol in your cocktails, with an increasing and varied number of non-alcoholic spirits to replace classic spirits such as gin, vodka and rum!

CONVERSIONS

In this book we have used a consistent 'measurement' throughout, or explanatory measurements where appropriate. We have included a conversion chart below to help you with convert to your prerred unit. However, what's important in most cocktails is the ratio, so if a cocktail requires 1 measure, ½ measure or 2 measures, you can easily use 1oz, ½ oz and 2oz or 25ml, 12ml and 50ml. The end product will taste the same.

MEASURE	OZ	ML
¼	¼	7
⅓	⅓	9
½	½	13
⅔	⅔	17
¾	¾	20
1	1	25
2	2	50

DRINK RESPONSIBLY

Always drink alcohol responsibly and in moderation, knowing your limits and never on an empty stomach. In this book we've collated some amazing cocktails, some that are on the stronger side of the ABV line. Please be sensible when consuming large amounts of alcohol and if in any doubt refer to resources such as;

https://responsibledrinking.eu
https://www.drinkaware.co.uk
http://www.responsibledrinking.org
https://www.drinkinmoderation.org

ONLINE COMMUNITY

This book was created thanks to inspiration from the wonderful community at makemeacocktail.com - The World's Best Cocktail Resource. We'd love for you to share your creations from this book on social media or with us at Make Me A Cocktail. Show us what you create from the classics to the complex and the crazy!

Makemeacocktail.com contains thousands of recipes for you to try, but also has our unique My Bar feature, allowing you to enter what you have in your cupboards at home so we can show you what you can make from what you have. We'll even recommend what to buy next to increase your cocktail making potential!

Register online for free to join the community and you can start to create lists of your favourite cocktails. Subscribe to our bi-weekly ingredient deep dive and be part of our vibrant and welcoming online community. We created the site for people just like you, to help you create, inspire, and entertain friends and family alike with the wonderful cocktail concoctions you can learn to make.

 makemeacocktail.com
@makeacocktail
 /makemeacocktail
 /makemeacocktail
/makemeacocktail

Make Me A Cocktail has found a martini that truly smells and tastes like Christmas! Get ready to impress your guests this festive season, the Mince Pie Martini makes for a sophisticated way to celebrate!

MINCE PIE MARTINI >

● ● ○

INGREDIENTS
- 1 measure **Gin**
- 2 measures **Dark Rum**
- 1 measure **Sweet Red Vermouth**
- 100g **Sugar**
- 50g **Mincemeat**

METHOD
First make a mincemeat syrup for use in the cocktail. Boil 100g sugar with 50g mincemeat and 100ml of water. Bring to the boil before cooling and straining. This will make a fairly large batch that can be stored in the fridge for later use.

Take a cocktail glass and dampen the edges with the mincemeat syrup, before dipping in some mixed spice to rim the glass. In a cocktail shaker mix 1 measure of the mincemeat syrup with the gin, vermouth and dark rum with ice and shake for 10-15 seconds until the outside becomes frozen. Strain into the cocktail glass and serve.

JEAN GABIN >

● ● ○

Looking for a naughty festive night cap that wins over the traditional hot chocolate? This classic cocktail created in 1986 by Charles Schumann is the perfect choice!

INGREDIENTS
- 1½ measures **Dark Rum**
- ¾ measure **Calvados**
- 5 measures **Milk**
- 1 measure **Maple Syrup**
- Dash **Nutmeg**

METHOD
First heat up the milk slowly in a pan. In another pan heat the maple syrup, calvados and dark rum. Pour in the hot milk to the syrup, calvados and rum before mixing and serving in an Irish coffee glass. To finish, sprinkle some nutmeg over the top.

RUDOLPH'S RED NOSE

A winter take on the classic summer sangria but a little different to mulled wine, warm up those chilly winter nights and thaw those red noses with your friends and family.

INGREDIENTS

- 1 bottle **Red Wine**
- 200 grams **Brown Sugar**
- 50 ml **Triple Sec**
- 500 ml **Orange Juice**
- 1.5 litre **Cranberry Juice**
- 50 ml **Sugar Syrup**
- ½ tsp **Almond extract**
- Sliced **Orange**
- 1 **Cinnamon stick**

METHOD

In a large pan on a low heat, add the red wine, triple sec, orange juice, cranberry juice, sugar syrup and cinnamon, except the brown sugar and almond extract until it begins to steam, in about 7 minutes. Take off the heat, add the almond extract and brown sugar and keep stirring until they are dissolved. Serve in latte glasses or mugs.

CHRISTMAS PUDDING SOUR

Got some leftover Christmas pudding that no-one managed to squeeze in after a mammoth Christmas dinner? We have got the perfect use in this tasty take on the classic sour. The Christmas Pudding Sour never disappoints our gin loving friends and family at Christmas!

INGREDIENTS

- 1 measure **Lemon Juice**
- 2 measures **Gin**
- 2/3 measure **Sugar Syrup**
- 1 **Egg white**
- 25g **Christmas Pudding**

METHOD

You'll need to extract as much flavour from the Christmas pudding as you can before making your cocktail. Infuse the gin with the Christmas pudding for at least 30 minutes, ideally a couple of hours.

Once infused, simply add the gin, lemon juice, sugar syrup and egg white into a cocktail shaker with ice, shake hard for 10-15 seconds before straining into an ice filled lowball glass. Serve with an orange peel twist and enjoy.

FIVE NEW YEARS TIPS FOR AMATEUR MIXOLOGISTS

If your New Years' resolution is to learn how to mix cocktails like the professionals, then we are here to help! Here are some useful tips and tricks of the trade that you can use at home to create beverages worthy of the Savoy Hotel.

CREATE A LIST OF TEN COCKTAILS

Trying to learn hundreds of cocktails all in one go is only going to confuse and demotivate you. Give yourself a list of your top ten favourite cocktails and work on perfecting these before any others. Keep these cocktails simple to start with – you can build up to more difficult techniques and complicated recipes later.

GET EQUIPPED

In order to make cocktails like the pros, you will need to stock your bar with a few basic tools. Of course, a bottle opener and corkscrew are essential, but you will also need to invest in a strainer, stirrer, muddler, mixing glass, jigger and bar spoon. It would also make sense to start collecting the various different types of glassware required for your cocktails of choice.

THINK QUALITY OVER QUANTITY

When you first set up your bar, it can be tempting to fill it with lots of spirits and liqueurs to make it look authentic. However, if you have a list of ten cocktails that you are trying to perfect, you can build your bar up gradually, purchasing only the ingredients that you will need and choosing a better quality of beverages in order to ensure yours is the home bar that everyone is talking about!

LOOK TO THE GARDEN

Some of the best mixologists use ingredients that they have plucked fresh from the garden, giving their drinks an organic, delicious taste that is hard to replicate with older produce. If you are able to grow some of your ingredients, then it should be a priority. In the meantime, always choose the freshest fruits, herbs and garnishes that you can, and never be tempted to opt for frozen fruit unless the recipe calls for it.

PRACTICE MAKES PERFECT

There are some mixology methods that are almost impossible to get right first time. If you have never muddled herbs before, it can be easy to over-stimulate them so that they over-power your drink. The key is to be gentle, muddling for just a few seconds in order to release the natural oils and delicate scents. Equally, using egg whites in cocktails is something that not everyone can master, as they tend to need a good, strong, shake for over ten seconds to get the light, frothy consistency that you need. Remember not to lose heart and keep practicing – it will be worth it in the end.

The path to mastering mixology might not be easy, with a few bad cocktails along the way, but once you know how to create your favourite drinks, you will never look back!

Did you know that when a bottle of champagne is opened, a Champagne cork can reach a speed of 24.8 miles per hour. Smashing!

FRENCH 75

Named after a weapon in World War 1, the kick from tasting the French 75, a highly decadent champagne cocktail, felt like being hit from said weapon! We felt it was a classy and luxurious way to enjoy champagne with our household favourite; gin!

INGREDIENTS

- ½ measure **Lemon Juice**
- 1 measure **Gin**
- ½ measure **Sugar Syrup**
- 4 measures **Champagne**

METHOD

Stir the sugar syrup, lemon juice and gin into an ice-filled Collins glass. Strain into a champagne glass and top up with Champagne. Garnish with a lemon slice.

WHITE LADY ›

This classic cocktail is like snow in a martini glass. With sharp citrus flavours using common ingredients found at home, it makes a great change to rich flavours synonymous with winter and Christmas.

INGREDIENTS

- 1 measure **Cointreau**
- 1 measure **Lemon Juice**
- 1½ measures **Gin**
- 2/3 measure **Sugar Syrup**
- 1 **Egg white**

METHOD

Add the Cointreau, gin, lemon juice, sugar syrup and egg white in a cocktail shaker with ice. Shake well for 10-15 seconds or until the outside of the shaker becomes frosted. Strain into martini glass.

CHOCOLATE ORANGE COCKTAIL

Christmas flavour combinations don't come much closer than chocolate and orange, right? Well we have found a way to enjoy such a rich combination of flavours as a cocktail. No more melted chocolate fingers sharing a segment of our favourite chocolate this Christmas!

INGREDIENTS

- 1 measure **Vodka**
- ½ measure **Orange Juice**
- 1 measure **Creme De Cacao**
- 2/3 measure **Orange Syrup**

METHOD

First rim a cocktail glass with sugar syrup then dab onto some grated dark chocolate. Simply add the vodka, crème de cacao, orange juice and orange syrup in a cocktail shaker with ice. Shake for 10-15 seconds until the outside of the shaker becomes frosted. To serve, strain into the rimmed cocktail glass.

BLACK RUSSIAN

The Black Russian first appeared in 1949 and is ascribed to Gustave Tops, a Belgian barman, who created it at the Hotel Metropole in Brussels in honour of Perle Mesta, then United States Ambassador to Luxembourg. As Russia is one of the coldest countries in the world, this classic cocktail is a must to wake up and warm the senses in winter.

INGREDIENTS

- 2 measures **Vodka**
- 1 measure **Coffee Liqueur**
- Top up **Coke**

METHOD

Pour the ingredients directly into a lowball glass with ice. Top up with coke. Stir and serve.

WHITE RUSSIAN

The White Russian is a potent, indulgent classic cocktail best served in a low light, low key, intimate setting. Father Christmas would need a designated driver or a taxi to deliver the rest of the presents after one of these!

INGREDIENTS

- 2 measures **Vodka**
- 1 measure **Cream**
- 1 measure **Coffee Liqueur**

METHOD

In a lowball glass with ice add the vodka and coffee liqueur. Give the mixture a stir to combine the ingredients before adding the cream on-top. Don't stir the cocktail before serving, and it should create a slightly layered effect.

GOLDEN DREAM ⌄

● ○ ○

The blend of orange, vanilla, cream and spices makes the Golden Dream a deliciously decadent yet different cocktail of Christmassy flavours. Best served in a martini glass, but can also be served over a large block of ice.

INGREDIENTS

- 1 measure **Galliano**
- 1 measure **Cointreau**
- 1 measure **Orange Juice**
- 1 measure **Cream**

METHOD

Add the Galliano, Cointreau, orange juice and cream in a cocktail shaker with ice. Shake well for 10-15 seconds or until the outside of the shaker becomes frosted. Strain into cocktail glass.

The Disaronno team believed the Godfather was a favourite of the great Marlon Brando, who, of course, played Vito Corleone in the movies of the same name. The true origin of this potent cocktail however remains a mystery!

GODFATHER ⟩

● ○ ○

Sultry winter settings, roaring fireplaces and surrounded by nearest and dearest. The perfect setting for The Godfather, a classic cocktail mixing two intense ingredients over ice. This famous cocktail makes for a great after dinner digestif.

INGREDIENTS

- 1 measure **Amaretto**
- 3 measures **Scotch Whisky**

METHOD

Simply add the ingredients over large blocks of ice in a lowball / old fashioned glass. Give the mixture a stir and serve.

BRANDY ALEXANDER

Brandy, chocolate and cream. Three flavours synonymous with winter and festive indulgence. The sprinkle of nutmeg or a cocktail glass rimmed with nutmeg and cocoa powder make for an exquisite finish sure to impress your guests or Insta feed!

INGREDIENTS

- 1 measure **Brandy**
- 1 measure **Creme De Cacao Dark**
- 1 measure **Cream**
- Grating of **Nutmeg**

METHOD

Add the brandy, Creme De Cacao and cream into a shaker with ice. Shake for 10-15 seconds until the outside of the shaker becomes frosted. Strain into a martini glass. Garnish with a sprinkle of nutmeg on top.

LIMONCELLO SPARKLE

● ○ ○

Champagne is the classic extravagant beverage to toast a special occasion. A Limoncello Sparkle takes this classic to a citrus and impressive new level. A wonderful alternative to the Kir Royale.

INGREDIENTS

- ½ measure **Cointreau**
- 1 measure **Limoncello**
- Top up with **Champagne**

METHOD

In a cocktail shaker with ice, shake up the limoncello with the cointreau, for 10-15 seconds until the outside of the shaker becomes frosted. Strain into a champagne flute and top up with the champagne. Garnish with a lemon peel twist and serve.

Did you know that Limoncello, which is mainly produced in Southern Italy, is made from the zest of a lemon, not the juice?

OUR TRADITIONAL CHRISTMAS COCKTAIL ROUTINE

Christmas in our house is not complete without an alcoholic beverage or two. There are so many drinks that we associate with the festive time, and we don't usually drink them at any other time of the year. Here are some of our household favourites.

MULLED WINE

This drink usually makes an appearance around Halloween and stays a staple in our home until the New Year. The smell of it seems to sum up the spirit of Christmas. If you don't want to try one of the recipes in the book to make at home you can buy it on the high streets in paper cups while you do your Christmas shopping. It is a true winter warmer, introduced to Europe by the Romans as they travelled through, conquering countries as they did so.

BAILEYS

We will be greeted with a glass of this when we first arrive at my mother in law's house. She always adds a dash of crème de menthe and crème de cacao to mine to turn it into a delicious After Eight.

MIMOSA

This may not be a drink that everyone associates with Christmas, but we certainly do which is why we had to include this classic cocktail in the book. Champagne and orange juice is the perfect combination for those who are designated drivers on the day. A cheeky little bit of bubbles at dinner is essential, and not too heavy with the banquet of food that will inevitably mean loosening my belt as we eat! Of course, there is little doubt that the Mimosa is simply a variation of the much-loved Buck's Fizz cocktail. The drink was named after the Buck's Club in London, and was invented as an excuse to start drinking early.

EGGNOG

This frothy drink tastes just like dessert, how Christmas should taste in my opinion. Sweet, creamy, and satisfying. I prefer a shot of brandy in mine (check out the Brandy Eggnog recipe), but my husband would rather have whisky. Eggnog was originally a British creation enjoyed by the aristocracy, but it is much more of an American tradition now. The Eggnog riot in 1826 happened when whiskey was smuggled into a US Military academy for a Christmas Day party. It cemented its place as a yuletide favourite.

PORT

When the cheese board comes out later in the evening, it is always accompanied by a bottle of Port.

Then, when the day is coming to an end, we always finish with a good coffee like the Christmas Coffee, the Mocha Eggnog Latte or the simple, good old fashioned Irish Coffee. The Irish Coffee drink was invented in County Limerick by a barman who worked at a pub near the airport. Some Americans disembarked their flight, tired, cold and miserable, so he added whiskey to their coffee to perk them up. It became popular at Shannon Airport and the recipe soon made its way overseas. It certainly warms and wakes us up ready for our long

Pears have a special place at Christmas, not only because of its significance in The Twelve Days of Christmas, but because it is a sweet, indulgent fruit that keeps for a long time once picked, so they were saved for special occasions over winter.

MULLED PEAR & CRANBERRY PUNCH >

There are so many wonderful alternatives to the traditional Mulled Wine in winter, we love how these warm winter cocktails can add something special to an occasion for being surprisingly different!

INGREDIENTS

- 1 litre **Cranberry Juice**
- 12 measures **Sloe Gin**
- 2 **Cinnamon sticks**
- 1 litre **Pear Juice**
- 2 **Vanilla Pods**
- 1 litre **Pear Cider**

METHOD

In a large saucepan add the pear cider, cranberry juice, pear juice, sliced vanilla pods and cinnamon sticks, except for the sloe gin and slowly bring to a simmer. Once simmering, leave for two minutes at a simmer for the flavours to infuse. Remove from the heat, stir in the sloe gin then serve. Garnish with cinnamon sticks and star anise.

CHAMPAGNE FLIP >

The Champagne Flip can be best described as the posh version of Eggnog you have likely never heard of. When we were sampling which recipes to include from makemeacocktail.com, this made the list as the wild card we think everyone should try at Christmas! Garnish with a grating of nutmeg or a sprinkle of cinnamon.

INGREDIENTS

- 4 measures **Champagne**
- ¾ measure **Brandy**
- ¼ measure **Orange Liqueur**
- 1 **Egg white**
- ¼ measure **Cream**
- ¼ measure **Sugar Syrup**

METHOD

Pour all the ingredients except the champagne into a shaker with ice. Shake for 10-15 seconds until the outside of the shaker becomes frosted. Strain into chilled champagne flute before topping up with champagne. Garnish with a grating of nutmeg.

B52

B52 is a classic shot; impressive looking, highly indulgent and the perfect drink to kick start or end a Christmas party!

INGREDIENTS

- 1/3 measure **Bailey's Irish Cream**
- 1/3 measure **Grand Marnier**
- 1/3 measure **Coffee Liqueur**

METHOD

Carefully layer the ingredients starting with the heaviest first which is the coffee liqueur, then the Baileys, and finally the Grand Marnier.

The B-52 was actually named after the famous band called the B-52s in the 1970's by a bartender who was a fan, contrary to the belief is was named after the B-52 bomber.

ST NICK'S FLIP

Cognac, muscat, orange and spices shape this creamy cocktail, no wonder ol' St Nick flips out and needs a rest when he's had one of these!

INGREDIENTS

- 1½ measures **Muscat wine**
- 1 measure **Cognac**
- 1 measure **Double Cream**
- ½ measure **Sugar Syrup**
- 1 **Egg white**
- 1 **Orange**
- 2 **Cloves**
- Dash **Cinnamon**

METHOD

Add all the ingredients in a cocktail shaker with ice. Shake for 10-15 seconds until the outside of the shaker becomes frosted. Strain into a cocktail glass. For the garnish, sprinkle some cinnamon on top, and stud an orange peel with the clover before placing on the side of the glass. Serve and enjoy.

Pumpkins are a member of the winter squash family and feature heavily in American tradition during the winter. The Pumpkin Sour makes for a perfect homage to this highly versatile fruit!

PUMPKIN SOUR

The spiced pumpkin syrup makes for a wonderfully wintery twist on a classic sour for you to enjoy.

INGREDIENTS
- 1 measure **Lemon Juice**
- 2 dashes **Angostura Bitters**
- 2 measures **Bourbon**
- 1 **Egg white**
- 1 measure **Spiced Pumpkin Syrup**

METHOD
Combine the Bourbon, lemon juice, egg whites and pumpkin syrup in a cocktail shaker with ice. Shake then strain into a rocks filled rocks glass. Garnish with ground nutmeg, a cherry and the dashes of Angostura Bitters.

FRENCH HORN >

Chambord is a highly popular liqueur at Christmas and New Year celebrations. The French Horn makes for a sophisticated yet simple alternative to the classic Cosmopolitan!

INGREDIENTS
- 1 measure **Vodka**
- ½ measure **Lemon Juice**
- 4/5 measure **Chambord**

METHOD
Chill the cocktail glass while making the cocktail, and once chilled rim the glass with salt. Shake the ingredients together in a cocktail shaker with ice, for about 10-15 seconds until the outside of the shaker becomes frozen. Strain into the chilled rimmed cocktail glass.

MUDSLIDE

The Mudslide is a classic cocktail combining rich flavours, that although it was allegedly invented in a bar in the tropical Cayman Islands, the rich combination of ingredients ensured its inclusion as a cocktail to enjoy at Christmas. To truly appreciate the Mudslide as intended it must be served as cold as possible.

INGREDIENTS
- 2 measures **Bailey's Irish Cream**
- 1 measure **Tia Maria**
- Top up **Chocolate Milk**
- Squirt **Double Cream**

METHOD
Shake the Bailey's and Tia Maria in a cocktail shaker with ice, for about 10-15 seconds until the outside of the shaker becomes frosted. Strain into a lowball glass and add the desired amount of chocolate milk. Finally add some squirty cream on top.

WINTER SIDECAR

If you're looking to hold and sip a little winter work of art, and fancy something different to the usual vodka, gin and whisky cocktail bases, the Winter Sidecar is for you! This cocktail was created in the Make Me A Cocktail online community by G Gallo.

INGREDIENTS
- 2 measures **Cognac**
- Touch **Cinnamon**
- 1 1/3 measures **Martini Bianco Vermouth**
- 2/3 measure **Clementine Juice**

METHOD
Roll the rim of the cocktail glass in water, or for an extra jazz some sugar syrup / orange juice. Once moist, roll the rim in the cinnamon to create a cinnamon rim to the glass. Shake the cognac, bianco vermouth and clementine juice in a cocktail shaker with ice, shake for 10-15 seconds until the outside of the shaker becomes frosted before simply straining into the cocktail glass. Garnish with a sprig of rosemary to awaken the senses.

CHAMPAGNE COMME-IL-FAUT

We're not sure if the linguists amongst you would agree with the naming of this perfectly balanced non-alcoholic cocktail, nevertheless it delivers on taste and is perfect for that early Christmas morning for all the family.

INGREDIENTS
- ¾ measure **Pineapple Juice**
- 2 measures **Ginger Ale**
- 1 measure **White Grape Juice**

METHOD
Pour the white grape juice and pineapple juice into a pitcher half full of ice. Top up with the ginger ale and stir. When serving, serve into champagne flutes and garnish with your favourite fruit, or for a festive feel rim the glass with coconut shavings.

MELNYK FLIP

○ ● ○

We debated whether we should include a cocktail with beer as an ingredient, however the unusual base makes for an earthy, rich taste accompanying the sweetness of the vermouth, bourbon and honey and felt the Melnyk Flip is best enjoyed when it gets cold outside. The original recipe asks for a great hoppy IPA beer.

INGREDIENTS

- 2 measures **Beer**
- 1 measure **Sweet Vermouth**
- 1 measure **Bourbon**
- 1 measure **Honey Syrup**
- 1 dash **Angostura Bitter**

METHOD

Add the Angostura Bitter, bourbon, honey syrup and Sweet Vermouth to a cocktail shaker with ice. Shake well for 10-15 seconds until the outside of the shaker becomes frosted and strain into a lowball glass. Pour in the beer and garnish with a cinnamon stick.

For a cocktail to be called a Flip, the recipe must use beer or an egg, sugar and a spirit (most commonly whisky, rum or brandy) or fortified wine. They were traditionally served warm however it's now more common to find Flips served cold.

BFG

The BFG, created by Adam Elmegirab, was the winner of the UK Drambuie Cocktail Competition 2010. In his cocktail the bitter used was one of his own creations entitled Dr Adam Elmegirab's Boker's Bitters. The warming spirits used in this award winning cocktail makes it perfect for chilly winter evenings.

INGREDIENTS
- ½ measure **Whisky**
- 1 2/3 measures **Drambuie**
- 1 measure **Sweet Vermouth**
- Dash **Angostura Bitters**

METHOD
Simply add all the ingredients into a mixing glass with ice. Stir for 10-15 secs and strain into a cocktail glass. The exact recipe for this drink used Noilly Prat Rogue, 10 year old Laphroaig and 2 dashes of Dr Adam Elmegirab's Boker's Bitters.

THE SUGAR TO MY SPICE
ACCOMPANIMENTS TO WINTER WARMERS

Nothing sums up Christmas better than warming winter cocktails. The smells, the tastes, the sensation of toasty warm indulgence create moments to savour. We have provided a little inspiration for accompaniments to enjoy with your satisfying glow.

GINGERBREAD
Whether it's breaking a piece off the Christmas gingerbread house, or picking up a perfectly iced gingerbread man, gingerbread is a wonderful biscuit for winter. We find gingerbread pairs beautifully with coffee based warm cocktails such as the Christmas Coffee or the Mocha Eggnog Latte.

MINCE PIES
Shortcrust, crumbly pastry, filled with sweet and spiced fruit mix, baked before eating and dusted with sugar make mince pies a wonderful treat to enjoy with any winter warmer. Jean Gabin, Santa's Stiff Hot Chocolate or a non alcoholic Pumpkin Latte work wonderfully well! Mini mince pies are the preferred choice in our house, you don't feel so guilty having a second or third!

STRONG CHEESE

The potent, decadent flavours of spiced and fruity winter warmers such as Glühwein or Mulled Pear And Cranberry Punch call for strong, rich and sharp flavoured accompaniments. Strong cheeses such as stilton, manchego, gorgonzola or pecorino are great choices but see what lesser known or regional alternatives you can find for a truly indulgent moment!

PICKLED FISH AND CRACKERS

For a traditional Scandinavian twist on the enjoyment of a mulled winter warmer, it must be paired with pickled fish, vegetables and crackers. The classic combination is pickled herring on rye crispbread or you could try pickled beetroot with smoked salmon on a seeded cracker. The stronger the flavours, the better the pairing with mulled winter cocktails such as Glogg or Glühwein.

GLÜHWINE

Mulled Wine, called "Glühwein" in German, is a traditional, spiced, warming Christmas drink in Germany and the perfect treat for cold winter days. You can buy mulled wine at every German Christmas market, but how about making your own at home?

INGREDIENTS
- 1 Bottle **Red Wine**
- 10 measures **Brandy**
- 3 measures **Anisette**
- 1 measure **Lemon**
- 3 measures **Orange Juice**
- 3 tbsp **Sugar**
- 6 **Cinnamon sticks**
- 8-10 **Cloves**

METHOD
Pour the red wine into a large pan and warm up over a low heat. Add the brandy, cinnamon sticks, whole cloves, sugar and anisette. Heat thoroughly, then add the sliced oranges and lemon. Cook the mixture over a low heat for about 30 minutes, but do not let it boil. If you would like it sweeter, add further sugar a teaspoon at a time to taste. To serve, ladle the drink hot in prewarmed glasses or mugs. Garnish with orange slices or a cinnamon stick and enjoy your traditional German mulled wine.

Glühwine literally translates to 'Glow wine' named unsurprisingly after that warm, comforting sensation you feel after a hot mug of this must-have seasonal drink. Glühwine is more commonly known as Mulled Wine.

To mull means to warm, sweeten and add flavour to a drink with spices and sweetness. We have provided you with the traditional German recipe, but you can experiment with different spices to find your preferred signature taste.

BITTER ORANGE & CARDAMOM MARTINI

Infused with the wonderful aroma of orange and spices reminiscent of Christmas, this delightful martini will be sure to get any festive party started!

INGREDIENTS

- 2 1/3 measures **Vodka**
- 1 measure **Cointreau**
- 4 tbsp **Lemon Juice**
- 1 tbsp **Marmalade**
- 2 **Cardamom pods**

METHOD

In a saucepan add the marmalade and heat up gently to make the marmalade runny. Do not let it boil. Add in the cardamom pods and crush to release their flavour. Let it heat through for a couple of minutes before taking the saucepan off the heat and leave it to cool.

Once cooled add the Cointreau and lemon juice to a mixing glass and add in the marmalade cardamom mixture. Stir to combine, ensuring you mix the liquids well with the marmalade.

To serve, take a chilled martini glass and add a dollop of marmalade to the bottom, before pouring in the mixture. Serve with a cardamom pod floating on top or an orange segment on a twizzle stick.

SANTAS STIFF HOT CHOCOLATE

We like to think this is Santa's favourite drink to come home to after a hard day's work out in the cold winter's night delivering presents. Mrs. Claus kept the recipe a secret.... until now!

INGREDIENTS

- 1 tbsp **Honey**
- 2 measures **Dark Rum**
- 2 cups **Milk**
- Couple drops **Vanilla Essence**
- 3 tsp **Brown Sugar**
- 1 **Cinnamon Stick**
- ½ cup **Grated Chocolate**

METHOD

In a saucepan over a low heat, add the milk, honey, sugar and cinnamon stick. Grate the chocolate into this mix and cook until the chocolate is melted. Don't rush and heat up the milk too quickly, or you risk burning the milk and not infusing the flavours enough.

Once melted, take off the heat to add the vanilla essence and the rum. Whisk the mixture before straining into the glass. Garnish on top with some whipped cream, mini marshmallows and chocolate shavings to serve.

Ginger is a spice frequently associated with winter and Christmas for its warming, fiery taste and uniquely rich scent. It is also synonymous with gingerbread men and gingerbread houses, a firm feature in households over the festive period.

SASSY LITTLE ELF >

For those who really want to impress their guests at Christmas with something a little different! X-Rated Fusion Liqueur is an unusual vodka based liqueur blended with exotic fruits with a striking pink colour!

INGREDIENTS
- 2 measures **X Rated Fusion Liqueur**
- 1½ measures **Guava Juice**
- ½ measure **Lemon Juice**
- 1 measure **Half And Half**

METHOD
Shake the X Rated Fusion Liqueur, guava juice, lemon juice and Half and Half in a cocktail shaker with ice. Shake well for 10-15 seconds or until the outside of the shaker becomes frosted. Strain into cocktail glass. Garnish with a lemon rind twist and a mini candy cane.

MOSCOW REINDEER COCKTAIL >

The heat of the fiery ginger beer and vodka, mixed with the coolness of crushed ice and mint make this simple cocktail a winter winner at any time of the day!

INGREDIENTS
- 2 measures **Vodka**
- ¾ measure **Lime Juice**
- 8-10 **Mint Leaves**
- 6 measures **Ginger Beer**

METHOD
Muddle the mint leaves in the bottom of a lowball glass with a little crushed ice. Add a little more crushed ice before pouring in the vodka and lime juice. Top up with ginger beer, garnish with a couple of mint leaves and biodegradable straw before serving.

WHISKEY MAC <

We asked one of our grandmothers what her favourite cocktail was at Christmas. She said Whisky Mac. Whisky and ginger, two fiery ingredients completing the most simple of winter cocktails to warm yourselves up on a cold evening. Thank our grandmother!

INGREDIENTS

- 1 measure **Ginger Wine**
- 1½ measures **Scotch Whisky**

METHOD

In an old fashioned glass carefully pour the Scotch whisky and ginger wine. Allow them to mix but don't stir.

TEQUILA WINTER > SUNRISE

When the cold nights and winter draws in, we sometimes yearn for that summer sun to come back round quickly! This slightly more adventurous take on the classic Tequila Sunrise should help you bring the sunshine to any occasion in winter!

INGREDIENTS

- 1 measure **Tequila**
- 1 measure **Orange Liqueur**
- 2 measures **Orange Juice**
- 2 measures **Cranberry Juice**
- Squeeze **Lime juice**
- 1 measure **Pomegranate Syrup**

METHOD

Pour the tequila, then the orange liqueur, orange juice and cranberry juice into a hurricane glass with ice (in that order). Gently pour the pomegranate syrup into the glass, before adding a squeeze of lime. Serve with a biodegradable straw and wedge of orange or slightly cheesy umbrella.

44

WARM BOURBON CIDER

We at Make Me A Cocktail are a fan of the quick to make drinks for lots of friends, that adds a little something special to a party. Winter parties aren't winter parties without something warming to drink, so why not try something different to Mulled Wine!

INGREDIENTS

- 2 tsp **Grated Ginger**
- 2 tsp **Grated Nutmeg**
- 3 measures **Whiskey**
- 2 **Cinnamon sticks**
- 1 litre **Apple Cider**

METHOD

In a large pan, combine the apple cider, cinnamon, nutmeg, and ginger. When the liquid is hot but not boiling, remove from heat and add your bourbon whiskey of choice. Stir to distribute the spices and divide this warming winter drink amongst your heat resistant glasses of choice.

SANTAS NIGHTCAP

A sweet and indulgent cocktail created at the Mandarin Oriental in New York City. Perfect for a cold winter nightcap to end an evening or party.

INGREDIENTS
- ½ measure **Kahlua**
- 2 measures **Dark Rum**
- 1 measure **Half And Half**
- 1 measure **Chocolate Chip Cookie Syrup**

METHOD
Add the dark rum, Kahlua, Half and Half and chocolate chip cookie syrup in a cocktail shaker with ice, shake well for 10-15 seconds until the outside becomes frosted, before double straining into a cocktail glass drizzled with chocolate syrup. For added flair at Christmas, garnish with some chocolate pearls and red coloured sugar to rim the glass!

WINTER PIMMS PUNCH <

⬤ ◯ ◯

Punch style cocktails are low maintenance for a party with many guests to cater for and still look like you have made an effort! We love to serve the Winter Pimm's Punch warmed, in different jars filled with punch and rustic fruit garnishes for a homely, winter party feel. This adaptable cocktail still tastes great served cold with lots of ice.

INGREDIENTS

- 500 ml **Brandy**
- 500 ml **Pimm's No. 1**
- 1½ litres **Apple Juice**
- Halved and sliced **Orange**
- Halved and sliced **Apple**
- 2 **Cinnamon Sticks**

METHOD

If serving warm, combine the brandy, Pimm's, apple juice, orange, apple and cinnamon in a large pan, heat but do not let it boil or simmer. Then, combine all ingredients in a sturdy pitcher, stir and serve. If serving cold, combine all ingredients into a pitcher or punch bowl with lots of ice and stir well before serving. Delicious!

CHRISTMAS >
COSMOPOLITAN

⬤ ⬤ ◯

Loved the world over, this Christmas take on the classic Cosmopolitan keeps the spirit of the original drink true, while adding some warming notes from the ginger and the gin.

INGREDIENTS

- 1½ measures **Vodka**
- 1½ measures **Gin**
- 3 measures **Cranberry Juice**
- Couple slices **Fresh Ginger**
- ½ measure **Lime Juice**

METHOD

In a mixing glass with ice add in a couple of slices of fresh ginger, before pouring in the vodka, gin and cranberry juice. Next add the juice of half a lime and stir to combine and chill, before straining into a chilled cocktail glass.

ALL THAT GLITTERS...
CHRISTMAS PARTY COCKTAIL

A few years ago, my sister in law and I sat in our compulsory festive knit, glass of warming mulled wine in one hand, trusty pen in the other, and began to write a list of all the food and drink we needed to make our upcoming Christmas party for all our frinds and family the best one yet! But... how do we make our Christmas Party that little bit special?

To show our love and appreciation to all our friends and family, we wanted to create a cocktail no one would have had before, that looked and tasted like Christmas! First, we chose our favourite base, champagne! We simply had to make a Christmas champagne cocktail, it's the perfect party drink, a symbol of celebration!

What about a Christmas Kir Royale? Yes, instead of crème de cassis we could swap with cranberry liqueur?! Adding a splash of cranberry liqueur to our champagne base in our favourite champagne flutes to create our Christmas cocktail. The sweet and tartness of the cranberry liqueur with the bubbles and finish of the champagne was an instant winner!

To finish, we added a few frozen cranberries and sprinkled a little edible glitter for that never-ending shimmer with the bubbles. In our opinion, the Christmas Baubbles Cocktail has become the ultimate family Christmas party drink and a tradition ever since.

The beauty of gaining confidence with cocktail making is that your creativity could create a new hit with friends and family! Imagination, a little confidence with the basics and a little desire to experiment is all that's needed to create a variation on a

PIMPED UP PROSECCO ⌄

This fruity prosecco-based cocktail makes a great alternative to Bucks Fizz on the morning of Christmas Day!

INGREDIENTS
- 2 measures **Orange Juice**
- ½ measure **Lime Juice**
- ½ measure **Pomegranate Juice**
- ½ measure **Elderflower Cordial**
- ½ measure **Passionfruit Juice**
- ¼ measure **Grapefruit Juice**
- Top up **Prosecco**

METHOD
Squeeze the orange, lime, grapefruit and passionfruit juice into an ice filled cocktail shaker. Follow with the pomegranate juice and elderflower cordial. Shake for 15-20 seconds or until the outside of the cocktail shaker gets too cold. Evenly distribute the fruit mixture between two or three champagne flutes. Top up each glass with prosecco, garnish and serve.

For a non-alcoholic alternative of Pimped Up Prosecco, swap the prosecco for lemonade. For extra indulgence, swap prosecco with champagne.

CHRISTMAS SNOWBALL >

Advocaat and Babycham are two retro ingredients that make for a delightful old-school combination with ginger syrup dutifully titled the Christmas Snowball. Enjoy!

INGREDIENTS
- 1 measure **Advocaat**
- 1 measure **Ginger Syrup**
- Top up **Babycham**

METHOD
Rim the highball glass with water and then sugar (or for added flair we suggest Christmas sprinkles). Into a cocktail shaker with ice, add the ginger syrup with Advocaat and shake for 10-15 seconds until the outside of the shaker becomes frosted. Strain into the ice filled highball glass and top up with the Babycham.

BABY BELLINI ∨

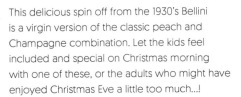

● ○ ○

This delicious spin off from the 1930's Bellini is a virgin version of the classic peach and Champagne combination. Let the kids feel included and special on Christmas morning with one of these, or the adults who might have enjoyed Christmas Eve a little too much...!

INGREDIENTS

- 1 measure **Lemon Juice**
- 2 measures **Peach Juice**
- Top up **Sparkling Apple Juice**

METHOD

Pour the peach juice and lemon juice into a chilled champagne flute and stir well. Top up the glass with the sparkling apple juice, stir gently to combine, garnish with a peach slice and give to the eagerly awaiting (or hungover!) family member. Delicious.

Glogg is a winter staple in Scandinavian countries and has been since the 16th century as a way to endure the cold weather, particularly for those who had to travel through the cold, brutal elements.

GLOGG >

● ● ○

A traditional Swedish take on Mulled Wine, Glogg is an essential part of any lead up to Christmas in Sweden. Apparently Glogg parties are thrown almost every weekend during Advent!

INGREDIENTS

- 1 Bottle **Red Wine**
- 1 tsp **Grated Ginger**
- 3 tsp **Sugar**
- 1 **Cinnamon Stick**
- 15 **Cloves**
- 6 **Cardamom Pods**

METHOD

Simply add the red wine, sugar, ginger, cinnamon stick, cloves and cardamom into a suitable large saucepan and heat slowly until the flavours have all infused. Do not let the mixture boil. Ladle into quirky Christmas mugs or latte glasses, garnish

THE NORTH POLE

Legend has it this decadent Christmas cocktail fires up Saint Nicholas before he prepares for the Christmas season... or at least we like to think it does! This is a highly indulgent cocktail, so enjoy without thinking about the calorific content!

INGREDIENTS

- 1 measure **Kahlua**
- 2 measures **Vodka**
- ½ tsp **Grated Ginger**
- ½ measure **Sugar Syrup**
- ½ tsp **Vanilla Essence**
- 2 tbsp **Double Cream**
- 2 tbsp **Chocolate Syrup**

METHOD

In a cocktail shaker with ice combine the vodka, Kahlua, chocolate syrup, vanilla essence, sugar syrup and ginger. Shake hard for 10-15 seconds until the outside of the cocktail shaker becomes frosted. Strain into a chilled lowball glass filled with ice before gently pouring the cream over the curved side of a spoon so it sits on top of the cocktail.

WINTER WHISKEY SOUR

Need a sophisticated end to a dinner party or an evening with friends on a cold winter night? The heat of the whiskey and the ice-cold citrus is a sensational taste for the end of the night.

INGREDIENTS

- 2 measures **Bourbon**
- ½ measure **Orange Juice**
- ½ measure **Lemon Juice**
- ½ measure **Sugar Syrup**

METHOD

Fill a glass with crushed ice to let it cool. Add the bourbon whiskey, sugar syrup, orange juice and lemon juice into a cocktail shaker with ice. Shake well for 10-15 seconds until the outside of the shaker becomes frosted. Strain the mixture into the chilled glass. Garnish with a slice of orange peel and serve.

MIMOSA ⌄

●○○

We are not sure about you, but Christmas wouldn't be Christmas without a champagne flute filled with the almost compulsory, classic Mimosa in the morning to begin Christmas Day celebrations in style.

INGREDIENTS

- 3 measures **Orange Juice**
- Top up with **Champagne**

METHOD

Add in the measure of orange juice to the bottom of a champagne flute before topping up with chilled champagne.

The classic Mimosa has understandably been subjected to a few variations. Why not turn your Mimosa into a Grand Mimosa, which includes a teaspoon of Grand Marnier.

HOT PEPPERMINT > PATTY

●●○

The Hot Peppermint Patty is a great alternative after-dinner drink or finding your inner hygge in winter, taking a traditional hot chocolate and giving it a minty, alcoholic twist. Bliss on a cold winter's night!

INGREDIENTS

- 1 measure **Peppermint Schnapps**
- ½ measure **Creme De Menthe**
- ½ measure **Creme De Cacao Dark**
- 5 measures **Hot Chocolate**
- 2 measures **Whipped Cream**

METHOD

First make your hot chocolate base as normal with your favourite choice of hot chocolate. Once prepared, add the Peppermint Schnapps, the Dark Crème de Cacao, and Crème de Menthe. Stir gently to combine. Fill any available space with whipped cream and sprinkle some chocolate shavings or marshmallows as a finishing touch. Enjoy immediately while warm!

SNOWBALL

● ● ○

When you think of a classic cocktail for winter, the Snowball tops the list! This classic cocktail is made with equal parts Advocaat, lemonade and lime juice. Try not to adapt the recipe too far from the classic white colour of the snowball, because well, we all know not to eat yellow snow!

INGREDIENTS
- 1 measure **Lime Juice**
- 1 measure **Lemonade**
- 1 measure **Advocaat**

METHOD
Shake the lime juice and Advocaat together in a cocktail shaker with ice for 10-15 seconds until the outside of the shaker becomes frosted. Strain into the desired glass and top up with lemonade. Garnish with a little grated cinnamon to complete.

Created in the UK in the 40s, the Snowball really took off in the 70s. Then its reputation declined somewhat, as the cheapness and sweetness of the drink fell out of favour. However, in 2006, chef Nigella Lawson was responsible for a 40% rise in sales of Advocaat, and the Snowball was revived.

Meanwhile, in America, the Snowball has always been looked at with suspicion. There is something about the combination of egg and lemonade that seems to put people off. However, keep an eye out for this as there is a growing number of people that are keen to see it become just as popular in the States as it is in Europe.

CHRISTMAS PUNCH

Perfect punch for a Christmas party! The pomegranate and cranberry juice gives it a fruity festive flavour, while Vodka and Cointreau will warm the guests when they arrive from the frosty weather.

INGREDIENTS

- 2 measures **Vodka**
- 2 measures **Cointreau**
- 2 measures **Cranberry Juice**
- 2 measures **Lemon Juice**
- 1 measures **Sugar Syrup**
- 4 measures **Pomegranate Juice**
- 1 measure **Club Soda**

METHOD

Simply add all the ingredients into a suitably large festive bowl, adding the soda water last, before giving it a quick stir and taste. Garnish with cranberries and lemon slices. Give your guests lowball glasses filled with ice so they can help themselves and keep going back for more.

WHISKY, WHISKEY AND BOURBON

Whisk(e)y features heavily in Make Me A Cocktail At Christmas, as the spirit brings a warmth, strength and depth to make for a satisfying moment in winter. There are many different whiskeys that you can purchase, but in general there are four main categories of whiskey: Scottish, Irish, American, and Canadian.

Scottish whisky's are made from a process that uses peat in the malting of the barley. Malting is the process of drying the barley and then soaking it to make it sprout before drying the barley again. Since peat is used during this process, Scottish whisky comes out with a mossy or peaty flavor that can be very strong at times. Scottish whiskys may be single malt or blended; single malt simply means that the whisky comes from a single distillery whereas a blended Scottish whisky made from several distilleries.

Irish whiskey, like Scottish whisky, is primarily made from barley. However, when malting process takes place, no peat is used which takes away the earthy, moss flavor that is found in the Scottish whisky and produces a smoother tasting whis Also, like Scottish whisky, Irish whiskey can be single malted or blended, made one distillery or blended from several.

American whiskeys can also be made of barley, but the majority of American whiskeys are made from other ingredients. The American whiskey, Bourbon, is mainly derived from corn, which gives it a sweeter taste than other whiskeys. The American whiskey known as Tennessee whiskey is actually bourbon that has been filtered through maple charcoal before it is put into casks, giving it a distinctive smokey flavor that differs from regular Bourbon. American Rye Whiskey uses the rye grain as its main ingredient, which gives it a fruity and sometimes spicy flavor.

Like American Bourbon, Canadian whiskeys usually feature corn as the main ingredient and like whiskeys from all other countries, Canadian whiskeys may be casked differently to alter the final product. Oak barrels are usually used in all countries, but the barrels may be new, used, or even charred to give the final product distinct flavours.

The name for Whiskey is said to mean "the water of life", so experiment with different whiskeys in your cocktails this winter.

BRANDY EGGNOG

Love it or hate it, we had to include the classic Christmas cocktail Eggnog. Make Me A Cocktail likes to find recipes that take a little spin on a classic. Our favourite by far is the rich, aroma filled, Brandy Eggnog.

INGREDIENTS
- 1 measure **Brandy**
- 1½ measures **Milk**
- ½ measure **Sugar Syrup**
- 1 **Egg Yolk**

METHOD
There's nothing complicated or extravagant about this recipe; simply add the brandy, milk, sugar syrup and egg yolk into a cocktail shaker with ice and give it a good hard shake for 10-15 seconds. Strain into a nice lowball glass with a few ice cubes, sprinkle a touch of ground cinnamon if you desire and serve.

It is believed that Eggnog originated in East Anglia, UK. Another theory is that it is a derivative of the Posset, another milk-based cocktail. It was popular amongst the rich, who were the only ones who could get hold of milk and eggs at the time, before making its way to the British colonies in America in the 18th century.

Eggnog became associated with Christmas thanks to the eggnog riots at the United States Military Academy in 1826. Some of the cadets smuggled the ingredients into the barracks to make a special cocktail for Christmas Day. The act resulted in disciplinary action for many of the soldiers

CHRISTMAS COFFEE

Taking the classic Irish coffee and infusing with some wonderful Christmas flavours, the Christmas Coffee is a real treat with a real kick to serve at a relaxing Christmas breakfast, making it a twist to your morning tradition.

INGREDIENTS

- ½ measure **Cointreau**
- ½ measure **Creme De Cacao**
- 6 measures **Coffee**
- ¾ measure **Irish Whiskey**

METHOD

Make up your coffee as you like it, before gently pouring in the Cointreau, Creme De Cacao and Irish Whiskey. Serve as is, or add milk or cream to personal taste.

HOT BUTTERED ∨ RUM

●●○

The classic Hot Buttered Rum brings the feelings of the festive period to life with its rich rum-based deliciousness.

INGREDIENTS

- 2 measures **Dark Rum**
- Sprinkle **Nutmeg**
- Dash **Vanilla Essence**
- Teaspoon **Brown Sugar**
- Sprinkle **Cinnamon**
- Teaspoon **Butter**

METHOD

Add the butter, sugar, vanilla and the spices into the bottom of a coffee Irish glass. Mix well then add some boiling water with the rum. Give it a good stir to combine ensuring the sugar is dissolved, then serve.

Did you know that rum is the oldest spirit in the world? It's made from molasses or the juice of sugarcanes. It was also the first spirit to be drunk for pleasure and not medicinal purposes.

MARTINS RUM

●●○

This is a super simple cocktail that is easy to scale up in the pan and share with friends! Suitably cringey Christmas jumpers optional.

INGREDIENTS

- ¾ measure **Lime Juice**
- 1½ measures **Orange Juice**
- ¾ measure **Lemon Juice**
- 1¼ measure **Dark Rum**
- ¼ measure **Southern Comfort**
- ½ measure **Sugar Syrup**
- 1 Teaspoon **Sugar**
- 1¼ measure **151-proof rum**

METHOD

Wearing your Christmas knit, source a suitable saucepan and add the 151 Proof Rum, dark rum, sugar syrup, and the three juices. Heat up slowly, ensuring the sugar has dissolved and flavours bought together before serving. Simply pour into an Irish coffee glass and let the warm notes slide down.

PUMPKIN LATTE

When we think of winter, we think of hearty vegetables and comfort food. This is an alternative, thick, rich latte, a perfect non-alcoholic alternative to spice up a cold winter's day.

INGREDIENTS

- 15 measures **Milk**
- 10 measures **Coffee**
- 3 tbsp **Brown Sugar**
- Dusting **Cinnamon**
- 100g **Pumpkin Puree**

METHOD

In a large pan, mix the milk, pumpkin puree, sugar and ground cinnamon. Heat gently, whisking constantly until the mixture just reaches boiling point. Transfer the mixture to three Irish coffee glasses. To garnish, top the glasses with whipped cream and a dusting of cinnamon sugar.

MOCHA EGGNOG LATTE

The wonderful community at Make Me A Cocktail have taken the Christmas drink Eggnog and combined it with coffee and chocolate flavours for a delicious yet simple twist on a classic.

INGREDIENTS

- 1 measure **Espresso Coffee**
- 1 measure **Chocolate Syrup**
- Top up with **Eggnog**
- Finish with **Whipped Cream**

METHOD

Combine the syrup and espresso in a Irish coffee glass. Top up the glass with Eggnog and finish with whipped cream and a little grated nutmeg if you like.

OBAL'S TOASTED ALMOND

Almond, Kahlua and Baileys blend extremely well together in this highly indulgent cocktail that should be enjoyed over plenty of ice and sipping slowly.

INGREDIENTS

- 1 measure **Bailey's Irish Cream**
- 1 measure **Kahlua**
- 1 measure **Vodka**
- 1 measure **Amaretto**
- 1 measure **Milk**

METHOD

Pour all the ingredients in to a shaker with ice. Shake well for 10-15 seconds until the outside of the shaker becomes frosted. Strain into a chilled lowball glass over plenty of ice. If desired, add whipped cream to enjoy this highly decadent concoction.

CHRISTMAS BAUBBLES

Created at one of the Make Me A Cocktail's family Christmas parties, this has become a tradition to enjoy amongst friends and family which we wanted to share with fellow cocktail enthusiasts. Merry Christmas to you all!

INGREDIENTS
- 1 measure **Cranberry Liqueur**
- Top up with **Champagne**
- 5 **Frozen Cranberries**

METHOD
In the bottom of a champagne glass add the frozen cranberries and cranberry liqueur. Slowly top up with your favourite champagne (or prosecco), taking care not to let the bubbles over fizz. To serve, sprinkle a little edible glitter in to the glass; the bubbles in the champagne flute glitter like the Christmas baubles against the light on your tree!

INGREDIENT FREQUENCY

Although we recommend a good solid varied cocktail bar in our Key ingredients section (p5), below we show you the top 13 spirits or liqueurs used in this book. Being a Christmas themed book some ingredients will definitely appear more frequently than a generic cocktail book. If you want to make as many cocktails as possible from this book, this is a great place to start.

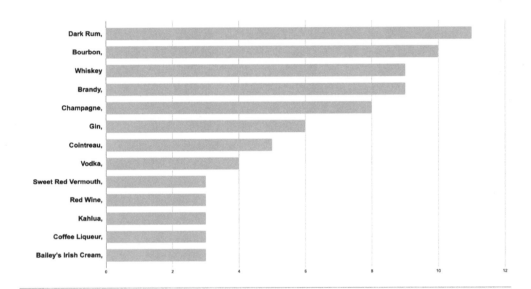

Along with the spirits and liqueurs, here are the top occuring bar stock ingredients from the book. We recommend having most of these in to give you the most options from this book.

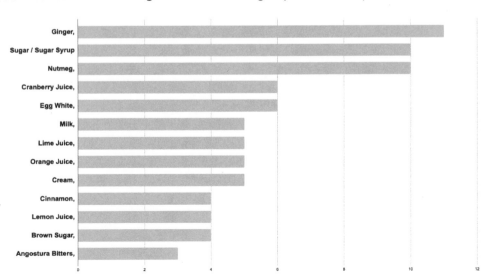

INDEX

INDEX CONT.

INDEX CONT.

CPSIA information can be obtained
at www.ICGtesting.com
Printed in the USA
LVHW070400141120
671609LV00008B/378

9 781838 262303